PRAISE FOR
Additional Possibilities for the Ark

In *Additional Possibilities for the Ark*, Anne Mugler orders the threads of her past, present, and future as carefully as she crafts her rugs; her choices hook us. The nuanced observations of a family systems therapist are evident in her crisp assemblages of particular words. Tightly condensed stories dissolve and re-form, varying like different dye batches of the same color. The elegant "Liminal Landscape" is painted with the spiritual tenderness of a watercolor. Even a piece as brief as "Complex Algebra" sparks travel beyond the limits of linguistic imagination, the last line a mantra. In the haiku, "This Is For You" she reminds us "no one goes to the desert unless they have to." No one could write such dense, spare poems having not spent time there.

— Sara Steele, water colorist and author of *Blueprints for Paradise*

Anne Mugler captures the universal themes of life that are woven into everyday experiences, and she does so with poignancy and humor—an artful achievement. Like the hooked rugs whose pictures are interspersed throughout the book, her poetry often has a folk art feel in its accessibility and lack of pretense. It's the kind of poetry that makes you want to pour a cup of tea and immerse yourself in the luxury of carefully crafted lines.

— Rebecca K. Leet, author of *Living with the Doors Wide Open*

With wisdom and stunning virtuosity, *Additional Possibilities for the Ark* is a direct path to the mystery of being alive. Anne Mugler's poems speak to what we know and what we don't understand and hold that tension together in beauty. Telling the stories of family, the ones that birthed us and the ones we live in now, the pain and loss, joy, and redemption, are woven together with carefully chosen stitches. She is a poet, therapist, and gifted rug hooker. Images of her rugs in this collection lift the genre to a higher level.

— Myra Binns Bridgforth, author of *No Sins of Omission*

An exploration of family, faith, and the way the mundane intertwines with the spiritual, *Additional Possibilities for the Ark*, provides a window into the soul of poet and rug hooker Anne Mugler that will have you reflecting on the beauty of your own life stories and lessons. Get ready to curl up and feast on the richness of the literary and visual art inside.

— Jennifer Lansbury, author of
More Than Words Can Ever Tell

Anne Mugler manipulates words as a fiber artist manipulates color—with clarity or subtlety, with mystery or directness, but always with intention. Both her poems and her rug hooking are done with deep artistic reflection.

— Nancy Slye, rug hooker and fiber artist

ADDITIONAL POSSIBILITIES FOR THE ARK

ADDITIONAL POSSIBILITIES FOR THE ARK
Copyright ©2022 Anne Mugler

ISBN 978-1-949652-17-8
Publisher Mercury HeartLink
Silver City, New Mexico
Printed in the United States of America

Cover photos and all interior photos by Turner G. Bridgforth

All rights reserved. This book or sections of this book may not be reproduced or transmitted in any form without permission from the author, except for brief quotations embodied in articles, reviews, or used for scholarly purposes.

Permission is granted to educators to create copies of individual poems, with proper credits, for classroom or workshop assignments, or reviews.

Mercury HeartLink: consult@heartlink.com

Mercury HeartLink
www.heartlink.com

ADDITIONAL POSSIBILITIES FOR THE ARK

Poems by
ANNE MUGLER

Mercury HeartLink
www.heartlink.com

CONTENTS

Preface xiii
Always Use Linen for the Backing of Your Rugs xv

ORIGINS

The Poultice.. 2
A 1948 Foodtruck... 3
Birth 4
Across Lines 5
The Braids.. 6
Roller Skate Lines 8
Blue Apron 11
Ishpeming... 12
My Midwest 13
What Dr. Mellancamp Tells Us Children 14
      In The Hospital
The Restaurant 16
I Rode Dressage 18
The Burial 20
Spawning Grounds 23
January 17, 2017... 24

CHANGES

Peace Terms	28
Summer Bouquet	30
Mechanics	31
Complex Algebra	32
Horses And Husbands	33
Terror	34
Reckoning	35
Body Blow	36
Vortex	38
Architecture	39
Introvert	41
Internal Punctuation	42
The Phillips Collection	43
The Fourth Wednesday In November	44
Molting	46
I Do Not Recommend Empathy	47
Ritual Of Return	48
Bodies Wear Stories	52

WHAT GIVES NOURISHMENT

Antiques	56
Lumbering Down To The Beach	57
Bad Boys Burritos Takeout Restaurant	58
Watching Soccer Through Fathers Who Are So God Damned Important	59
Joey	60
The Piper	61
Myriad Layers Map Out A Life	62
On Being Nursed Back To Health By My Mother After The Second Hip Replacement	63
Owen At Three Months	65
Feathers On The Ground	66
Owen Flies Down His Great-Grandmother's Hallway	67
Rat Poison	68
I Have A Wonderful Spot On The Top Of My Head	70
Liminal Landscape	71
This Is For You	72

SPIRIT

Additional Possibilities For The Ark 76
Baptism In California 77
Red Hibiscus, 2017... 78
Jungle Incarnation 79
Silence.. 81
Beginning.. 82
Meares Glacier.. 83
Dear Father 84
Orange Roses In A Vase.. 85

Acknowledgments And Thanks 86
List Of Hooked Rugs 89
About The Author.. 91

PREFACE

I have written all the poems and hooked all the rugs within this book. I am saved by the act of describing. Be it pen or hook, the move toward placing in space, a thought, memory, or vision is a grounding and reassuring experience. Once done the piece can be seen which allows me to go forward leaving a trail that describes a life.

I write to tell stories. I hook to actualize a vision. Both get the inside out and resolve something internal.

Art is made and offered to the world with hope that it begins a conversation between the artist and the observer. The artist flings her work out into the universe often not knowing what that conversation might be but with the faith that it exists. A poem or rug lives by companionship with the eye of the observer where there is a possibility of true exchange.

ALWAYS USE LINEN FOR THE BACKING OF YOUR RUGS
for Mary Sheppard Burton

said Mary, teacher of many truths.
It lasts decades, lifetimes, eternities.
Consider its durability—it wraps mummies
resists carpet beetles, resists moths.

Bast fiber of flax, stiffening stems.
Retted from the inner bark, scratched from the skin.
Get honest linen, Mary said, whose threads determine
a straight line, produce an evenness in hems

so you can believe your last loop will be
settled into the same line as the first
leaving a legacy of heckled fibers, rehearsed
cloth which holds the image only you can see.

Get honest linen from Belgium or Scotland or Italy
then pull your wool tight and remember me.

ORIGINS

POULTICE

I wrap tired arms around
my young son's body.
I angle my head to watch
the forming of his goofy grin.
He wiggles into my chest
shifting me back into another heart
soft like mine: the memory-hold
of my faraway mother
her blood-red poultice
wrapped around my aching arms.

A 1948 FOODTRUCK

The Huddle parked in front of the Luther Hotel
fed the small town bankers and high school kids
hamburgers and hand-cut French fries
made daily

by the young couple who got up
at dawn to peel potatoes and
shape meat into perfect circles.
They had honeymooned in Vero Beach

and never left.

The man had managed kitchens
on submarines, could cook quickly in quantities.
The woman hooked her star to his
knowing life would never be dull.

They became pregnant in 1948
welcomed the baby in 1949
in the midst of a hurricane.
The child did not remember the ceaseless wind

but to this day has an insatiable appetite
for very good French fries.

BIRTH

When I was born
you hid under the hospital bed
while a nurse took me away.
The 1949 hurricane was coming.
You thought I would be better off
with her.

I do not remember this.

But it is told over and over
by laughing family members
so I think I remember
being taken away from you

but I don't.
Rather the incident
is lodged in my bones
where longing for you
still resides.

ACROSS LINES

As a girl I spoke weekly by phone
to my grandmother in Oklahoma.
She had a body-worn hearing aid -
the earpiece connected
by a thin wire to the transistor
attached to the top of her slip.
To hear me she needed
to hold the phone receiver
next to the transistor.
I would wait in silence -
visualize my grandmother
holding the big receiver
down by her breast
believing she took in every word
through her heart.

THE BRAIDS

Eight years old, allowed
to walk home from school for lunch.
After eating, to walk my sister
to afternoon kindergarten.
Sister with the cute nose
bright blue eyes and
finest flaxen hair in the family.

More than anything
she wanted braids.
Mother accommodated
let the blond hair grow long
enough for two pigtails.
But plaiting them was another story.

Sister's hair, so fine, knotted overnight.
By morning was a crazy mess.
As mother started to undo the braids
from the day before
sister's whimpering commenced.

As mother gingerly combed out knots
screaming followed
first in squeaks, then in hollers.

Walking in the door for lunch
I stared at the sobbing fiasco
invented a huge space
between myself and those
two poor things trying so hard

saw what it meant
to want something so much
you endured pain
and to love someone so much
you gave it.

ROLLER SKATE LINES

A perfect quarter-circle
was created on our driveway
by the roller skate wheels our father
attached to the fence, built to cut that driveway

in half.

One half led to the sidewalk
where we chalked hopscotch squares
tossed carefully weighted keychains
prayed they landed on desired numbers.

The other half led to the garage
backyard, and vegetable garden.
I think the fence was built to keep in
our little brother and the dachshund

but I can't be sure because that dog
was always in trouble, running the streets
shitting where she wanted
which made our father say bad words every day.

Eventually we gave her to a better family
one who could at least train her
but we did not get rid of the fence.
So every night

we kids had to make sure
it was open by dinnertime on the days our father
came home for dinner, or he would get mad
have to get out of the car

do it himself, even though
the dog was gone, even though
little brother was bigger, even though
he'd been the one who'd put it up.

BLUE APRON

The bow tying my grandmother's apron
was the first thing I saw
walking into the kitchen of the cabin

where she fried the bluegills
I caught with my grandfather
after I ran down the steep hill

to our pier extending out
into Lac La Belle.

The lake provided hours of water play
in the blue canoe
kept at the bottom of the hill

where my grandfather taught me
to bait the hook for catching
our lunch, which he plopped

into a tiny bucket for me to carry
up the long climb to my grandmother
waiting patiently

in her blue apron.

ISHPEMING

Once I scrambled up waterfalls -
nine years old, all legs and arms
eyes on rushing water
hands on stones and boulders
tennis shoes on edge of rocks.
Ascending that descending stream
I believed those waterfalls
would take me to heaven.

That summer our father landed us
in Ishpeming, Michigan.
At age nine — with a father
who carted us from state to state
park to park, ocean to ocean
never tiring in his relentless
search for beauty — those waterfalls
were my salvation.
Alone with rushing water
away from his persistent drive
I scrambled heights
of my own making.

Now, seven times nine
writing near waterfalls in West Virginia
thumbing through dictionary, thesaurus
stunned to discover
that in Ojibwa, Ishpeming means Heaven
and remembering father
who for a moment
let me get there.

MY MIDWEST

Where mother would send me alone
to Peepers grocer with a dime for bread.
Where winters brought crystalline snow
so bright on sunny days, we were blinded
walking from school, and bundled head to toe
so damp when we got home
we simply steamed through the door.

Where dwellings were called
for decades by the family's name:
The Shambreck house where lived the boy
who dug to China when we were eight.
The Kurtz house where lived the children
so well behaved, mother stated
I think Mr. Kurtz drinks.
The Stickford house where lived the Catholics
the reason I was given
for their having eight children
all of whom slept in two, tiny bedrooms
of their Milwaukee bungalow.

When I was eleven my father put me
on one of the murky, yellow cars
of The Milwaukee Road — and I boarded

unaware childhood was ending —
with every click on the track
vanishing into the vapors
of the steadily moving train.

WHAT DR. MELLANCAMP TELLS US CHILDREN IN THE HOSPITAL

This is your brother, John.
You are going to like him.
He will stay a baby longer
which warmed my fifteen-year-old heart
because I wanted a real baby
not one to babysit, but one to feed
burp, believe was my own.

This is your brand-new brother, John.
He has special lines drawn straight across
his palms that will never go away
which I knew marked him
so I started to listen better to
Dr. Mellancamp who talked softly.

This is your brother, John.
He will not learn as fast as you
but he will smile and love you
which I did not understand but believed
because Dr. Mellancamp always told me
how brave I was after polio shots.

Some families put babies like John
in an institution but that is not happening
in your family. You will take him home
which relieved me because
there had been some rumblings
some unexplained tension between my parents.

*This is your brother, John,
one of the broken angels
who will not judge you
and with whom you will never argue.*
Which he did not say
but foretold just the same.

THE RESTAURANT

The reef, a quarter mile
off the coast from the family's restaurant
supports a habitat for
turtles, lobsters, corals.

Lodged on the reef
remains a wreck.
From shore it looks like a submarine
which launched the tall tale it was

a German vessel abandoned
after World War II
a reminder of victory or how close
we came to a different outcome.

The family has owned the restaurant
over fifty years —
an infinitesimal number
when compared to reef formation

but large
when compared to hours or minutes
it might take for increasing Nor'easters
or hurricanes to wipe out the place

made of driftwood
set on twenty-foot pilings in sand.
Winds might catch the roof
taking everything on the pilings out to sea.

The family willingly takes the risk
although it is said the patriarch
remains in a storm
his sense of oneness with the place

driving his resistance
to abandon the island
as if his presence would divert the winds
or hold fast the restaurant's roof.

Like waging a battle for love
even as the outcome is more and more
precarious.

I RODE DRESSAGE
for my brother, Charley

He was twelve when he told our mother
he wanted a horse. She told him

to get a paper route to earn
the money to feed it. So he did.

If he could have ridden his horse
to throw the news he would have.

In centuries past, he might have been
a pony express rider galloping across

the plains delivering the mail from
one end of the continent to the other

thrilled to be on time, thrilled to be alive
in a time when horses were the only

way to get anywhere. When stealing one
could get you shot, hanged, or otherwise killed.

But he delivered the news on his bike
which allowed him to feed his horse

which led him to other horses
fine quarter horses, thoroughbreds, polo ponies

and cow ponies on whom he herded
cattle to clear the Gros Ventre range.

Once I rode his very first horse.
Galloping down a country road

I almost fell off. Loose legged and shook
I reined in my brother's mare. Dismounted.

Knew our callings would diverge.
He really was the cowboy.

THE BURIAL

I.
He was flown from the tropics to Idaho
then carted to Wyoming
five hours by car.

His final wish: to be buried next to his uncle
a physician who doctored on horseback
across the Popo Agie Wilderness
over the red rocks of the Wind River Range

through the sagebrush near the graves
of Sacagawea and her Shoshone brothers.
Painted horses grazed near infrequent streams
while the firmament, immense and challenging

covered the territory day and night
relentless blue, dazzling darkness displaying every star.

II.
He was laid to rest on a knoll
overlooking the valley of his ancestors.

His children having hauled him from humidity
now saw he was placed
in the depths of this country.
Southern Wyoming, an expansive country
for an expansive father.

III.
He had been in his grave for only a day
when a blizzard blew in from the western range
blinding the living who knew they must leave
or be trapped in the place of their father's desire.

Fleeing from town they were flagged at the edge
forewarned of a menacing swath moving towards them
black and determined, unnatural and strange
until it grew legs that held herds of black angus

trotting beside them with every intention
of taking the road to much lower pastures.
Cowboys on horseback drove cattle
toward siblings whose bodies recoiled in fear

as they waited to start their five-hour trek
as they waited to leave their determined father
now covered with that country
now covered by that country
now covered in that country
at the end of his day.

SPAWNING GROUNDS

I sold the house in Lander
the ornery father tells his second daughter.
Home of his uncle, aunt, cousins
his happiest history.

He will go to Milwaukee
to the springs of his success,
to where he made the money
     which became the pivot
     for all relationships that followed
to where he felt born.

I don't blame him. I have felt
the force of running salmon
bash aside my booted foot
seen the twisting, shimmering bodies
swim upstream through cold currents
lunge through paws of baby black bears
leap up waterfalls taller than men

to leave their life, to end their life
in the waters where they were born.

JANUARY 17, 2017

Today you would have been ninety-four
if you had lived, and some of your children
would be fretting about whether the money
which took care of you, would run out.

Others would be hoping you lived another year
so the gifting would continue.
You had the good sense to slip away in your sleep

during the shift of your favorite caregiver
who was not one of us, and before
patience, love, and money ran out.

On your birthday you used to say
you only wanted a card, and I would
scour the stores for the perfect one
never finding it.

After years, I settled on the most treacly
one in the rack. Going overboard
seemed the best bet for both of us.
I think you liked those cards

really believed the sentiment.
Today standing in the card aisle
of the grocery store, I spied one
that would have satisfied us both.

I read it out loud.
Did you hear me?

CHANGES

PEACE TERMS

Sarah went down to South Carolina
to confront her stepfather about his betrayal.
They had fired hostility at each other
for twenty years.
Said everything but the truth
about his hands ripping her flesh
about her wish to retaliate with murder.

The same day
I went down to Appomattox Court House
to listen to a Confederate boy
tell me about surrender.
Tell me about April, 1865.
Tell me about his legions marching
on a dusty road
into a sleepy Virginia village.
Lincoln said *Let 'em up easy, boys.*
Grant ordered them food.
Chamberlain commanded *Present arms.*
Gordon touched saber to boot returning the salute.
And the grey flag boy stumbled across
giving and clutching his charge
the cloth of his character catching his tears
the cloth of his character pried from his hands.

At home that night I hear
Sarah's stunned voice
across phone lines.
He apologized she whispers
He said he was young and dumb.

And I made terms —
never touch me again.

SUMMER BOUQUET

Mrs. Wells' Black-eyed Susans
are blooming today
dancing with the orange tiger lilies.
In early evening
I drive to the flower stand
to buy Black-eyed Susans and more
because I no longer live next to Mrs. Wells' garden.
I left last winter, did not say good-bye
could not bear another ending.

Now I miss her flowers and Mrs. Wells and you
whom I can never have as I now imagine.
You — like purple freesia, all sure of yourself
wanting me
and wondering why not.

Last night I built a bouquet
mixing freesia and Black-eyed Susans
purple and yellow, proud and tall
standing separately
with small daisies and the breath of babies
for support.

MECHANICS

The mare's right hind moves to the inside
when she is tracking right.
She arcs left widening the circle
to inappropriate proportions.
My legs, my voice, my hands
have no meaning on this curve.
Her pain, or the memory of it
dictates the dimension of her figure.

The car is making a funny noise
gasping for no apparent reason
somewhere to the right of the radio.
I practice the sound so I can
execute it for the mechanic.
Maybe he can adjust
the hose or the compression
or some hydraulic what's-it
I have no effect on

like my marriage which made
a funny noise
tracking to the left
tracking to the right
not responding to pressure
or mechanical expertise.
A hissing sound like a slow leak.

COMPLEX ALGEBRA

The man dictates an equation
of ultimatums and false values.
I bracket the limitations and
solve for what matters to me.

HORSES AND HUSBANDS

Today in the riding lesson
we worked on the extended canter.
At the signal, the mare recoiled —
her forward movement restrained
by my stiffened arms.

My trainer repeated
move your seat, give with your elbows.
Finally, we achieved several strides of extension.

I thought about the riding lesson
and tomorrow when I face you in mediation
when I must ride with sharp mind into the meeting
pride swallowed, humiliation set aside
so I might move forward with my life.

I stopped at Brown's hardware store
bought an Arkansas whetstone.
Nothing compares to the edge
achieved with an Arkansas whetstone.

Dropped it into my purse, a totem
to keep sharp my vision of extension.
Then drove home with the back-roll solid at my waist
preventing my spine from giving into its curvature.

TERROR

It was the shadow side of a moonlit wave
a black menace

mesmerizing, rising, rising
to terrifying crest
the height holding my breath

then to breaking — splitting sand

then to surf —
foam spreading gently over feet

What scared me so?
My heart pounded at the sight of the rising.

It merely flowed into softness
leaving just a trace in the sand.

No one, no one who had not been there
would believe what I saw.

RECKONING

I shall arise reluctantly this dawn
to figure out the waiting numbered sheaf.
I am determined not to be a pawn.

I start the calculations and a yawn.
The columned ledger acts as nighttime's thief.
I shall arise reluctantly this dawn.

I hope I don't go slack-jawed at the lines
or give this job away with feigned relief.
I am determined not to be a pawn.

I'm unaffordable was one foregone
conclusion. I refute this base belief!
I shall arise, reluctantly, this dawn.

Expendable, intractable, and overdrawn.
Enough! I say — hold tight this new belief:
I am determined not to be a pawn.

I leave behind these ruthless kings and queens
but if I am to bear the cost of grief
I must rise unreluctantly. This dawn
I am determined not to be a pawn.

BODY BLOW

We go to the movie to fill
the hours between poll closings
and results.

The internet reports:
seasoned, female politician
for President has
72% chance of winning.
Inexperienced, narcissistic
businessman has 28%.

The movie — MOONLIGHT —
"an unbearably personal...
episodic chronicle....
about the dignity, beauty,
and terrible vulnerability of
black bodies...
and the mysterious bond
that links us to one another."

Rising from MOONLIGHT
its poetry embedded
in our bones
we exit the theater
turn on our phones
stand speechless
in front of Target

bodies bent over
bludgeoned by words
on our screens:
inexperienced, narcissistic
businessman has won.

*quote from review of MOONLIGHT by A.O. Scott,
The New York Times, 10/21/16*

VORTEX

Barometric pressure
temperature
humidity
three conditions necessary
for a tornado.
And there lies unsuspecting Kansas
quietly tending her rows of corn
suddenly side-swiped
by the raging funnel
and wondering
> *what hit me,*
> *were my furrows crooked*
> *did I forget to check the Almanac*

or had nature
sucked her up
into a conjunction of conditions,
her only crime
her presence?

ARCHITECTURE

I collected coquina shells as a child.
Built castles and churches
with the white sands of Naples.
Sister would direct the design
carefully place my tiny shells
on the walls of the buildings.

Stained glass windows she would lean back and say.

Alone on Ocracoke Island
the beach teems with coquinas —
wiggling, determined cockles
gathering at my feet.
No sister here
directing this design.

I think of us
try to hold clear what we accomplished
left alone
as children
on those white sands
of Naples.

INTROVERT

I'm beginning to like the night
as much as Plath liked the oven.
No one comes at you and all
the blind-eyed beauty becomes
illumined by the dark.

INTERNAL PUNCTUATION

Last summer I asked
my high school English teacher
when do you use a semicolon?
Without hesitation she replied
> *internal punctuation*
> *elimination of the pause*
> *substitution for a conjunction*
> *recreation of a connection.*

For example, with two simple sentences, one might say
> *Alice is the one with the curious questions.*
> *Julie is uncomfortable with clarifying answers.*

Add a conjunction, there would be no pause
> *Alice is the one with the curious questions,*
> *and Julie is uncomfortable with clarifying answers.*

Substitute the semicolon for the conjunction
there is still no pause, but it would read
> *Alice is the one with the curious questions;*
> *Julie is uncomfortable with clarifying answers.*

See how the semicolon
redefines the bond?

THE PHILLIPS COLLECTION

I remember the day I bought
the print by Milton Avery
Greenwich Villagers
to replace a painting
lost to a separation.

Today I am perched
on the edge of a bench
staring at his *Winter Riders*
whose horses look as if
they are separating
two sets of forelegs
diverging off gray road

separating or perhaps yielding
towards the edge of the path.

THE FOURTH WEDNESDAY OF NOVEMBER

I can only say I'm grateful
for the friend who sat with me
in the hospital waiting room

and for the one who
organized meals to spare me
stumbling around the kitchen.

I can only share my gratitude
for the young technician
who found the tiny vein

on the outside of my right hand
so the IV could deliver
the propofol.

I can only offer profound thanks
to the surgeon who shouted to
my attending nurse

be sure to tell her
we got the two nodes
and they were clear.

And I can only shed grateful tears
for the tall, stately orderly
who helped me

put on my socks
wheeled me to the curb
lifted me into the car

whispering *happy Thanksgiving*.

MOLTING

Skin-shedding
such a messy business.

Dried up sheets of the past
cling to a glistening present

and I wriggle
like a slithering idiot
publicly peeling away

the lack of fit

forgetting in the moment
that transmutation
is my nature.

I DO NOT RECOMMEND EMPATHY

Just when I thought
we were getting
to the problem, I said
I really empathize with you.

As if I am the hands
in her gloves
or the feet
in her shoes.
As if I am her waist touching
the waistband just above
her undergarments
or her left ear perceiving
the timbre of birdsong.
As if I am her inner brain
releasing chemicals
when her child cries.

I am not her

and my empathy
full of hubris
as obstructive as
fog blinding vision.

She, who is fearful
needs to hear
the opposite of her fear
not its echo.

RITUAL OF RETURN

In 2020, a pandemic swept across the world. People shuttered their homes and locked out the world in an effort to prevent illness and death. Over 800,000 people died in the United States alone. This separation and loss created ordeals and challenges for everyone. After 14 months a vaccine was created allowing for a potential return. Everyone has a story about this time. This is mine.

I.
I would like to tell you about the separation.
I am in the Apple store buying a new laptop.
I exit the store leaving my old one
to transfer the information.
A young man comes running after me.
You must take both —
the old one and the new one.
We are closing the store.

They are closing the store.
They are closing the churches.
They are closing the schools.
They are closing the jobs.
I am closing my house.
People are dying.
Fast.

II.
The dark is immediate.
My sister gets it first.
Long hours in bed.
Night terrors.
Recovery takes months.

I write to observe myself
to know I am a self.
I buddy up with a friend
to keep that self sane.

Six months into it
I get breast cancer.
Two surgeries for removal
of evil cells.

Christmas brings my
two-year-old grandson.
It is like the coming
of the Christ child.

Yanked back
into loneliness.
Radiation.
Arms wrenched into
a steel straight jacket.

Darkness deepens.

Masks become gifts
enabling touch
from holy healers -
kind doctor
technician
acupuncturist.

My brother gets it next.
He is handicapped.
Rules let no one visit.
I pray
his radiant smile
is a balm to his nurses.

In the darkest days
I scream
Will I ever have people
in this house again?

III.
I get the shot.
I fly to Florida.
I tell the flight attendant
I am going home for my mother's 96th birthday
and burst into tears.

The attendant's kindness
outlines my body in new reality.

I am seen.
I am returning.

BODIES WEAR STORIES

the scar on the lip
from an overturned bike

the indentation in a finger
from a gold wedding band

the flawed fingernail
caught in the door

the limp of a man
who had polio at five

the turnout of a dancer
retired for years

the tattoos on the breast
guiding beams of light

WHAT GIVES NOURISHMENT

ANTIQUES

I sit on my screened porch
surrounded by treasures
bought or found
in places that hold
the possessions of strangers
and I wonder at the lives of those

who opened and closed
the wooden hutch
covered with green chalk paint
gotten on the Eastern shore
for my son who used it
as a bookshelf

and I remain grateful
for the sign found off
an obscure dirt road
in an old, dilapidated barn
smelling of leather and absent horses
hidden in the corner amongst
junk and mouse droppings

that reads GOOD LIFE COMPANY
which is what I have had
and so, maybe, had another
who created the sign to hang
above his office
years before I was born.

LUMBERING DOWN TO THE BEACH

dragging towels, sons, and nephews
I drop the whole lot and heave my body
down into a chair.

Leaning back, I absently finger
the sands of my childhood
lean over to look for a sea-gift.

Saltwater dribbles down my arm.
Sand flies — my silly nephew
has sprinkled me with attention before
running to find his own treasures.

I see the tiniest shell
one quarter the size of my fingernail
and as perfect as a newborn.

Silly boy runs back waving
an old, weathered nautilus
larger than his head
barnacled and grey.

I show him the tiny shell
stare at his old one.
Such a tender mercy.

BAD BOY BURRITOS
TAKEOUT RESTAURANT

A bench along one wall
green and low

dwarfed by a deli counter
Warm air from the open kitchen

Smell of frying green onions
Menu on chalkboard

reading *we roll phatties*
in organic flour tortillas

And a lady on a stool
saying *how can I help?*

WATCHING SOCCER THROUGH FATHERS WHO THINK THEY ARE SO GOD DAMNED IMPORTANT

I wait for phalanxes of self-importance
to fill, to close up ranks to block my glance.
I next prepare to bend my head because
askance is certainly the place to pause

to see through life dismissals. Then, I watch
my crazy son plow down the field of such
projected men, and with the grace that's just
his own, dives deep into the dark abyss

of unified distortion, weaves between
the shallow kicks, and he is fully seen
to fly with all the wit of angels 'round
the rage of aging arrogance. He's found

more strength that I in his brash breakaway.
I am glad I have come today.

JOEY

His mother asked me to take care of him
a toddler, for the weekend.

I was honored, hauled my two boys
to Florida to fulfill the request.

I was warned he was an active baby
walked early, was able to get anywhere

so I slept with him in his parents' double bed
just in case, just to watch over him.

Late in the night I heard a rustling sound
things being rearranged, and there was

no Joey in the bed. In terror, I rushed
to open the closet from which came the noise.

I spied him high up on a shelf smiling
like the Cheshire cat who always

freaked me out, and I breathed deeply
trying not to scream, trying not to

freak out little Joey who had managed
a feat of inexplicable acrobatics while

I was snoring away, dreaming that I
his watchful, organized aunt

had everything under control.

THE PIPER

I could have gone the other way
through Andrew's fields and Carlin's Glen
or climbed the hill to Carlin's Ridge
and followed the path to Four Mile bridge.

Instead, I took the lower trail
through roses barely blooming,
through laughing children twirling swings
through sweaty brothers shooting
hoops with fathers giving cheers and shouts
through mothers putting picnics out
piling high the wooden tables.

I heard him first before I saw
the piper playing beyond the bend
glancing at us as if he knew
his hopeful notes on Sunday's end
would tie us all together. Kin
in play and sport
and food and song
held in grace, almost in prayer
by piping notes, by blessed tune.

MYRIAD LAYERS MAP OUT A LIFE

He has lived on many streets
so the white-out in my address book
resembles a salt and flour map

a geographical formation

that begins to rise
just below the A in his first name
until it thickens, becomes uneven

trips the pen as it rolls over the next address.
There is strength in the white thickness
until it craters where the typography

cracks just over the final number
in a recent zip code. A white mound punctuates
the last line, a large drop one might climb

before sliding down to fresh paper
which holds the foreign address
of his present home.

ON BEING NURSED BACK TO HEALTH BY MY MOTHER AFTER THE SECOND HIP REPLACEMENT

This is how my sister describes our mother's skills:
good cook, no nonsense, fairly perfect nurse
best during late night flu sessions and

the required regimen for getting back to normal
first warm coke, then one saltine, then jello
followed by baked potato, no butter.

I would add to the list: sits without complaint
on required raised toilet seat, entertains
by attracting feral cats with chicken nibblets

has breakfast ready whenever one sits at the table
toast still warm, cereal unsoggy
orange juice cold, coffee hot

plays well alone with computer games
provides evening entertainment by mixing
PBS news with gin martinis

tops Florence Nightingale, beats the Red Cross
rivals Percoset, and I am seriously considering
having a third hip replacement.

64 What Gives Nourishment

OWEN AT THREE MONTHS

The sideways glance
caught by the camera
reminds his great aunt
of his father.

I think the eyes resemble
his mother's mother.

But what I also see
is how deep they are.
How someone so small
looks like he is thinking

already forming
an opinion of the history
into which he is born —

generations of merchants
scientists, dancers, curators
renegades, revolutionaries
sureties of the Magna Carta —

all those lifespans
all those prototypes
all those possibilities
present in his small self

sitting in his mother's arms
surrounded by love.

FEATHERS ON THE GROUND

Yesterday
a drive to Broadway, Virginia
time with Nancy Slye on her farm
sheep, cattle, goats
muscle-necked llamas
who nuzzle my cheek.

I pick up feathers at Nancy's farm
peacock, quail, guinea hen, duck.
The larger ones for quill pens
to dip into ink
to give to Sunday School children

to write like sages and monks
like the scribes of Israel
to write their own prophecies
stories, scriptures
or words of a Messiah.

OWEN FLIES DOWN HIS GREAT-GRANDMOTHER'S HALLWAY

and won't stop. He has escaped.
His chubby legs have learned to run.
This infinite corridor is his joy.

Passing door after door
he races into the giant lobby
surprises residents
who love him
though he could knock them down
like ten pins.

His destination:
water fountain with loose rocks
painted seasonal colors.
He grabs, two-fisted.
Plants rocks at the feet
of now watchful residents.

His great-grandmother
rounds the corner, spies him.
Ninety-three years separate them.
They see each other
burst out laughing.
Another tender mercy.

RAT POISON
for Meg

Near the bottom of the grocery list
after the broccoli and toothpaste
you have written: rat poison.

I imagine that is deliberate
that you meant to intentionally
print those clearly formed letters

which accumulate into two startling words
ones that could shift the boredom of food shopping
into a creative or scary endeavor.

Or maybe it is to remind you that the world
is never quite so simple — in the same store
you can find stuff to nourish you and to kill you.

But knowing you, it is meant to remind us
that the grocery list is never quite complete
never perfect — which is annoying

but essential to living a life in which
we are not worrying about coming home
with enough broccoli or toothpaste

but with a sense of humor
laughing at the ridiculous notion
that we really are in charge

that everything is always
in the right place

including the rats.

I HAVE A WONDERFUL SPOT ON THE TOP OF MY HEAD

which my acupuncturist calls
Hundred Meetings

the closest point to heaven
where the ancestors dwell.

Maybe that's why
I've become heir

to family pictures, ancestral charts
and ancient Bibles.

I like to peruse
the old photographs.

Whenever I have troubles
I look to the sky and say

Come on everybody.
Carry me, you darlings.
I need you.

LIMINAL LANDSCAPE

Thin space
of well-being
or deep discomfort

carried so keenly
it can be conjured up
in the body

moss under foot
birdsong clipping air
crackle of fire

night as quiet
as the silence
preceding creation.

THIS IS FOR YOU

yellow-dotted mug
broken Haviland teacup
unpacking heirlooms

purple candles burn
sixteen sweet rolls on the stove
sing we now of Christmas

blind to our efforts
mice scurry past all the traps
right before our eyes

unyoked, wandering
no one goes to the desert
unless they have to

pale orange cloth
oval table with brown bread
eat, this is for you

SPIRIT

ADDITIONAL POSSIBILITIES FOR THE ARK
for Connie

Two oval eggs in the mourning doves' nest.
Twin Texas highways divided by bluebonnets.
Boy and girl babies in sweet Margaret's belly.
Unmatched socks under two single beds.
Blue leather cowboy boots worn at the toes.
Braces on brothers bespeckled with pimples.
Manatees mating beneath still waters.
Two little sisters refusing to pose.
A child and his nurse raising bread to the gulls.
Trembling hands rounded slightly in prayer.
The backs of a couple bent over in age.
A prism of light arching twice through the air.

I tell you this now, this is how it's been coming:
promises, covenants rolling in pairs.

BAPTISM IN CALIFORNIA

The weeping headlands of Encinitas
carve fonts of stone, basins for baptism.
Heaven's water pools and waits.
Who will cup the gathered drops

and drown my brow in forgiveness and grace?
Where is the baptist whose birth prepared
the way for such a day of water-cut stone.
A day for being born again, for washing all

the wrongs away, for headlands dripping
to rolling seas, and me, caught somewhere in between
now kneeling, then drowning in all the hope
these waters bring. I dip my hands

in shallow pools and drip the waters
upon my brow, forgive myself for all
my sins, close my eyes and begin to bow
to the weeping headlands of Encinitas.

RED HIBISCUS, 2017

Three blooms burst.
Sizzling plates of happiness
rising audaciously from dry earth.

    Almost sixteen years ago
    I walk down Wall Street

    embers hiss
    cathedral-shapes burst forth
    grey smoke rises from scorched earth.

    Privileged to stand
    on hallowed ground
    I do not visit the site again.
    Let the dead rest.

Blooms tumble to the ground
return to earth
reseed.

JUNGLE INCARNATION

Dark river in Costa Rica
Slow moving fog, sporadic rain.
Pontoon boat gliding silently
> Watch for the Jesus Christ lizard.
> He will become afraid
> and walk on water.

Scanning, scanning for
green animal in greener jungle

then motion

creature rises up on hind legs
skin flaps spread between toes
long tail steadies for balance
> and the Jesus Christ lizard
> sprints across the water.

I gasp.

Did the Twelve take such a breath
when they saw Him crossing
luminous and demanding
not through gentle rain
but raging storm?

Did He feel afraid
imagine a predator
at His back?

SILENCE

All leaving depends on Harriet separating from Henry
whose hind legs no longer support his canine body.
Nova Scotia is calling. Harriet's response is silence.

The shepherd leads them to greenery and still waters.
Children follow, shout at danger stalking lost sheep.
Grown-ups stare, ponder heaven in silence.

Everything depends on leaving by two o'clock
before the blind-eyed busyness begets delay
the appointed time to retreat into silence.

The shepherd would lay down his life for his sheep.
No words ever spoken, no questions ever asked.
Who among us can live in the core of that silence?

Everything depends on Harriet leaving Henry
who may die, unattended, in the days after
departure, forsaking Harriet for silence.

In the beginning of heaven and earth there were no words.
How did God stand the deafening stillness?
Children know He is in them, even in the silence.

BEGINNING

Boy and girl twins meet grandmother at her funeral.
They are barely a year at first glimpse of her.
Is death always present at every beginning?

The thirteenth fairy gets no invitation.
Silence breaks forth for one hundred years.
Must darkness be summoned to all our beginnings?

Mary wonders and weaves for weeks
Bearing weight that grows daily inside her.
At the end of the journey comes the Beginning.

We have named autumn fall. Rilke says,
Each leaf falls as if it were motioning 'no.'
And all must descend to nurture a beginning.

The young man's perfection is unsustainable.
His heart stops at the truth, his mind is far behind.
He does not know that loss precedes this beginning.

We kill for reasons beyond our comprehension.
Depravity is a warping, continuous error not isolated
      or named.
We must talk about sin. We must begin at the beginning.

MEARES GLACIER

The nations raged, the kingdoms moved;
He uttered his voice, the earth melted.
                              Psalm 46:6

The air sharpens, the water thickens
to aqua silt.
We are borne before you
brilliance arranged at the top of the world.
And you are coming —
blue-veined bergs, waterfall veils
cloud-covered shale
an advent so dazzling
we become ignorant from distraction

until you silently drop your own substance
awaken us with your roar
force us to be vigilant for all the acts of
        your conversation.
There is an arc of pronouncement between the
        separation and the final plunge.
In the time between the calving
and the thunderous result
all could be forgiven.

DEAR FATHER

You were so hard on us.
We could not fix your loneliness.
But on the days you could give us
your tenderness
on the days you called me Annie
with all the love you could muster
on those days —

well, they were something
and they crept into my skin
left an internal tattoo.
It simply took
those pure
few markings
given every so often
to know my own goodness.

ORANGE ROSES IN A VASE

Ask the question
If my dead father were here
what would it be like

He is dead
You can eat with his fork
or pick up your own

Even after burial
ghosts can still come to dinner
Do not set a place

Just asking the question
changes the order of courses
the number of them

Come to my dinner
bring orange roses in a vase
We can rearrange them

ACKNOWLEDGMENTS AND THANKS

Thank you to the following publications in which these poems or earlier versions have appeared:

Gauntlet of Dreams: "Vortex", "Molting", and "Introvert"
Passager: "Additional Possibilities for the Ark"

I am fascinated by stories. I am indebted to the storytellers in my life: Rabbi Edwin Friedman who spun fables about humans and the Rev. James Sledge who told stories of humans and their God, my psychotherapy clients who bravely brought their lives to my office and my friends and family whose stories and lives are deeply woven into my own.

I am very grateful to the poets I have known and worked with: to Henry Taylor, Ed Hirsch, and Billy Collins for brilliant classes, to Tim McDermott for the long hours sitting in Borders Bookstore workshopping poems, and to my poetry group, Myra Bridgforth, Rebecca Leet, Ann Rayburn, Mel Snyder, and Jeremy Taylor. All have been my teachers, and I am indebted.

I give grateful thanks to my rug hooking group, the Lambs, taught by our teacher, Mary Sheppard Burton who told us we were all artists and could design anything if it came from the heart. All the Lambs rose to her belief and are fine dyers and hookers of wool. They include Lucy Clark, Channing Huhn, Harriet Lynn, Carol Mabon, Patt Madlener, Dolly Rowe, Nancy Slye, and Allene Thibeault.

Thank you to the Lost River Retreat Center located in the wilds of West Virginia. Many of these poems were written, revised, or read at the Poets&Writers&Artists retreat I co-lead there twice a year. The roaring fire in the stone fireplace and the wonderful meals provide a nurturing backdrop for creativity.

Special thanks to Turner G. Bridgforth for his beautiful photography and excellence in the digital world. His fabulous assistance in compiling this book is only second to his kindness.

I am blessed to have wonderful friends. Thank you, Meg Wallace for best words, Cynthia Lovell for Bible Dog, Sara Steele for beauty, Myra Bridgforth for wonderful collaboration, Patt Madlener for Tuesdays, Carmen Pierce for comfort, Jenny Lansbury for faith, and quite a few more who create and share their tables with me.

My mother is a fine writer. If you see her byline, you know there is a cleverly written story about to be told. My father's life created countless stories, some of which are in these poems. My parents' lives and their love of me gives me courage.

Finally, my sisters and brothers, sons, daughter-in-law, nephews, and grandson provide memories, old and continuing. A deep sense of love comes from being in their presence. They inspire me.

LIST OF HOOKED RUGS
All rugs executed by Anne Mugler

Cover   Vertical Crow, Horse, and Duck (original by Magdalena Briner Eby, 1832-1915)

p. xvi   Home (Original artist unknown)

p. 10   Bear Walking (Original by Anne Mugler)

p. 22   House with Path (Original artist unknown from Forager House Collection)

p. 26   Compass (Original artist unknown, circa early 20th century)

p. 40   New York Geometric (Original artist unknown, circa 1885 from Barbara Carroll)

p. 54   Boys on the Hill (Original by Anne Mugler)

p. 64   Checkerboard (Copied from painted wood, original artist unknown from private collection)

p. 74   Navajo Chief Blanket, second phase with block patterns and concentric squares, 1865-1879 (Original artist unknown from collection of William Randolph Hearst)

p. 80   Multicolor Star with Clamshell Corners (Original artist unknown, circa 1880-1890, from collection of Shelburne Museum)

ABOUT THE AUTHOR

Anne Mugler lives in Arlington, Virginia where she works as a psychotherapist in private practice. She began her life in Vero Beach, Florida and moved with her family back and forth between points in the Midwest and the waterways of Florida. She began doing needlework at age seven, taught by her grandmother. At twelve, she found herself at summer camp composing lyrics to camp songs. She began her career as a special education teacher before going to the University of Chicago to become a family therapist. Her love of poetry and the fiber arts came together after her two sons were born. She began writing short lullabies and decorating her home with very simple rugs. Her first rug is one of her boys standing on the hill in their back yard. For years she rode horses where she found the same joy in the precision of dressage as she did in the precision of poetry and rug hooking. Her poems and essays have appeared in journals and artbooks. She has hooked rugs for over thirty years, dyeing her own wool and often designing her own patterns. She is particularly drawn to designs of unknown rug hookers who have gone before. She co-leads Poets&Writers&Artists retreats in the wild mountains of West Virginia.

Made in the USA
Middletown, DE
21 June 2022

67462667R00062